The Red Door
A dark fairy tale told in poems

Shawn C. Harris

Ben Yehuda Press
Teaneck, New Jersey

THE RED DOOR ©2022 Shawn C. Harris. All rights reserved. No part of this book may be used or reproduced in any manner whatsoever without written permission except in the case of brief quotations embodied in critical articles and reviews.

Published by Ben Yehuda Press
122 Ayers Court #1B
Teaneck, NJ 07666

http://www.BenYehudaPress.com

To subscribe to our monthly book club and support independent Jewish publishing, visit https://www.patreon.com/BenYehudaPress

Jewish Poetry Project #29   http://jpoetry.us

Ben Yehuda Press books may be purchased at a discount by synagogues, book clubs, and other institutions buying in bulk. For information, please email markets@BenYehudaPress.com

Cover painting by Alaina Otto

ISBN13 978-1-953829-34-4

22 23 24 / 10 9 8 7 6 5 4 3 2 1   202220729

Dedication

*Dedicated to my father,
Herman Leon Harris.*

May his memory be for a blessing.

Contents

BOOK ONE: BEREISHIT (IN A BEGINNING)

kaddish	2
klippot (empty shells)	4
arrival	5
tzfat	6
days	7
the red door	9
rose	10
she loves monsters	11
monster	12
haunting	13

BOOK TWO: YETZER HARA (THE EVIL INCLINATION)

the city of two faces	16
monsters everywhere	17
prowl	18
a small token	22
kiss	23
the better to know you with	25
names	26
scar	27
dreams	28
beware beware	30

BOOK THREE: SITRA ACHRA (THE OTHER SIDE)

the palace	34
gifts	35
silver candlesticks	36
why why not	38
fragile	39
home	41
bloody kisses	42

agony and ecstasy	43
warning	44
the red door opens	45
akeidah	46
hineini	48

BOOK FOUR:
GALUT
(EXILE)

awakening	52
changes	53
red dreams	54
medusa	55
breathe	56
the visit	57
chrysalis	58
déjà vu	59
monster's lullaby	60
four answers	61
reawakening	63

BOOK FIVE:
TESHUVAH
(RETURN)

a wedding	66
unanswered	67
kiddushin	70
nightmare	71
song of tirzah	73
metamorphosis	74
forgetting	75
bittersweet	76
a mother's lament	77
come and see	78
About the Author	79

Book One:

Bereishit

(In A Beginning)

kaddish

flurry of fat feathery snowflakes
falling onto half-frozen soil
cushioned in the womb of the earth
dad slumbers in his pine box bed
until the world to come

    we are but dust and ashes v'imru amen

mourners clad in black gather round
the open mouth of dad's resting place
rabbi spins a sermon to soothe
sharp edges left behind by loss
fist after fist fills with cool damp earth
black dirt splays across pale wood
in the ground under their feet
the dead whisper secrets from beyond

    we are but dust and ashes v'imru amen

a mother and three children
two sons and a daughter
missing a dad
pieces of him spread all over them
oldest son's brow and jaw
younger son's nose and ears
daughter's sterling silver star of david
dull golden gleam of the widow's wedding ring
one day they will all dwell here
in their own wooden houses

    we are but dust and ashes v'imru amen

they sit shiva in mom and dad's house
it's just mom's house now
in the kitchen a potluck banquet of comfort food
greetings and condolences
from aunts uncles cousins friends
trickle into the daughter's ears
she sees empty sockets where eyes should be
from their mouths worms and moths spill out
arms that hug are gleaming white bones of skeletons
lips that smile are macabre grins of bleached skulls

we are but dust and ashes v'imru amen

klippot (empty shells)

black ants marching one by one
across an orange peel
oblivious and brief
one by one puny bodies march
toward the gap in the cement
disappearing into the abyss
the peel left behind
an empty shell of a world

earthlings live toil die eyes shut tight
eat sleep work fuck buy pray
more more more faster faster faster
killing time killing themselves killing each other
the nothingness inside them grows
until they return to the dust
of their hollow world
such is life they say
smiles brittle as eggshells

two women lie nude in bed
share the remains of a rolled cigarette
what's going on
behind those dreamy eyes of yours
asks she with the dirty blond nest of hair
what's her name again
she crowned with a halo of thick coarse hair
searches the expanding darkness of her pupils
seeking soul sparks stardust something
but only finds eyes vacant as a doll's
all smooth surface containing nothing
another empty shell

empty shells, she says
everything is empty shells

Shawn C. Harris

arrival

at ben-gurion airport
here she comes hauling her baggage
rendered clumsy by her burden
beneath smooth brown skin
beneath halo of coarse dark hair
the plantation and the shtetl
live in blood and memory

her passport names her
tirzah persephone horowitz
after an aunt on her dad's side
who died so young in the camps
and her mother's favorite greek myth
but to call her tirzah is too much
like uncovering her nakedness
like speaking aloud the holy name

what shall we call her
to keep secret those pieces of herself
she keeps separate and sacred
shall we call her terry
terry sounds nice
sweet simple syllables
fit like a tailored garment
concealing her mysteries

tzfat

i am ancient guardian
watching over surrounding hills
buildings of pale stone clinging
to my wind-swept mound

i am a city of song
plucked strings of a lyre
loud brassy klezmer
throbbing techno beats
shoes clop-clopping on cobblestone
tires screeching on the asphalt river
winding round my peak

i am temple made of air
city of priests inhaling holy words
sacred prostitutes exhaling hookah smoke
breathing life into my streets
baruch shem kavod malchuto l'olam va'ed

i am gathering place for the unseen
departed spirits wandering alleyways
delivering cold shivers to the living
stray cats peeking from gathering shadows
eyes glimmering gemlike in meager light
demons on bodies of dust and air
rising from deepening shadows and stagnant pools
street lamps and porch lights shining
electric fireflies swallowed in my darkness

days

under a cocoon of covers
she sleeps off the jet lag
dreaming of red things
candied apple
rose in bloom
blood dripping
a door opening
(come and see come and see)

it was evening then it was morning
her first day

she calls her mother
(such a nice jewish girl)
and they talk
everything and nothing
at the center of their speaking
a silence shaped like dad

it was evening then it was morning
her second day

she descends toward the realm of the dead
men in big black hats and big black beards
flock around tombs slathered in sky blue
crows squawking prayers
fingers pecking pages of psalms
the dead slumber in beds of stone

it was evening then it was morning
her third day

she is a ghost haunting quiet corners
of cafes restaurants bookstores
people cast her strange looks
where her eyes see man woman child
others see only empty space

it was evening then it was morning
her fourth day

during a twilight interlude
she watches a demonic horde
swarm the streets in feline shapes
feast on treasures from the trash
hissing curses
glaring at humans with the evil eye
(chamsa chamsa chamsa chamsa chamsa)
crouching shadows swell in size
waiting to pounce

it was evening then it was morning
her fifth day

at a glassblowing workshop
students roll red hot glass
into mezuzah covers
seder plates
wind chimes
kiddush glasses
she stares at the round, hollow shape she made
wonders what it could be

it was evening then it was morning
her sixth day

and on the seventh day
she rests

Shawn C. Harris

the red door

palace of wind and shadow
ghostly white curtains
blowing
soft as final breath

a corridor the color of night
song of unbodied voices
haunting
irresistible

door as red as ram's blood
silent as a tombstone
waiting
patient as the grave

come and see come and see

rose

beyond the red door
on the other side of sleep
terry walks through a garden
vast and barren as a desert
corpse cool breeze caresses living flesh

nothing living grows
only scrawny, ugly trees
twisted limbs and branches grasp like claws
wrinkled bark casts shadows like faces
gaping in horror glaring in anger grimacing in pain

splash of color draws her eye
statue half shrouded in shadow
some kind of devil demon or satyr
cloaked in powdery dust white as bone
fingers wrapped around a single rose
red as blood red as heart's desire

curious fingers graze warm soft petals
pulsing faintly like a tiny heart
a thorn bites into a thumb
dark red drop drop drops to the earth

terry wakes up
crimson trail across her hand
jagged cut on her thumb
she licks the wound
tastes iron and salt
and the faint flavor of flowers

she loves monsters

terry loves monsters
loved them since she was a little bitty thing
watching that cartoon for the first time
you know the one
about the mermaid
the witch
and some prince
eyes glued to the screen for the witch's scenes
fascinated captivated enchanted
but the witch must always die
and this made terry sad
though she could not say why

terry loves monsters
loved them since her first pimples and pubes
sneaking dracula under the covers
wondering what it would be like
to feel a vampire's fangs on her neck
to taste human blood in her mouth
to transform into wolf or bat or mist
but dracula always dies
staked and beheaded by good christian men
because magic and mystery must not survive

terry loves monsters
loved them since she was in undergrad
viewing Cocteau's masterpiece for a film course
imagining herself in Beauty's place
living with the Beast in that wonderful castle
running her hands through thick soft fur
staring into eyes like matching gold rings
snuggling against the beast in the big canopy bed
naked or clothed as you please
but the Beast must always become a Prince
wild things must be tamed

monster

on the other side of the red door
terry wanders her dream garden
heady musky scent
ancient raw primal
luring her to its source

something has changed

in the place where her blood spilled
wild grass and tiny flowers grow
rosy aroma merges with mating season smell
entices terry's senses
once again she reaches for the rose

it happens so quick

a deafening *crrrrrack!*
chunks of stone falling
hot iron grip seizing
monstrous silhouette
eyes like twin yellow moons

terry breaks away and flees

running running running
don't stop don't stop don't stop
legs aching lungs burning
the monster getting closer closer closer
its breath upon her hot and alive

she wakes up

tangled in her bedsheets
sweaty breathless aching all over
just a (rose) nightmare (monster)
nothing to worry (red door) about

Shawn C. Harris

haunting

in dreams terry visits her dad
lays a stone on father's grave
uproots weeds clinging to the headstone
hiding his name
hiding his memory
judah horowitz
was yehudah ben natan
beloved husband and father

terry brushes away
dry leaves and loose dirt
hiding his name
hiding who he was
judah horowitz
had lion's paw hands
that could kill a man
yet handled fragile things
so delicately
like glass and people and hearts

taloned hand erupts from the ground
captures terry in deathlike grasp
she screams and screams
crying out
dad father aba daddy
earth splits open and swallows her
down
down
down
she goes into its yawning maw
into the cold and dark

Book Two:

Yetzer Hara

(The Evil Inclination)

the city of two faces

i am the city of two faces

one face i show you
the face of travel guides and listicles
for tourists and expats
sight-seers and other visitors
just passing through
snapping selfies on cobblestone streets
filling cafes and art galleries
gulping watered-down kabbalah

this is the face i let you see

my other face I hide
behind spray-painted chamsas
warding off the evil eye
inside the mouths of old women
spitting *ptuh! ptuh! ptuh!*
to keep misfortune at bay
behind the fervent prayers of the pious
at the graves of mystics and sages
in the waters of stagnant pools
and the shadows of palm trees
where sheydim and unclean spirits lurk

this is my true face

monsters everywhere

she sees the monster everywhere

in the amber light of a yellow moon
glowing yellow eyes gazing hungrily

in the whiff of floral perfume
the fragrance of roses and pheromones

in the cloud that floats above tzfat
a clawed hand reaching for her

in the winter wind rustling dry leaves
panting breaths stroking the back of her neck

in the shadows cast by people and animals
a shape half human and half beast silently stalking

in the dark chaotic depths of her dreams
a steely grip pulling her through a red door

prowl

somewhere in the artists' quarter
terry comes to hide
in people in booze
in the hellfire glow of dirty lights
in the sweet burning smell of hashish
she is invisible
safe

the air is feverish thick wet
a jungle heat
clogged with perfume and pheromones
pounding techno beat
terry blends into smoke and noise

terry sees her
lounging by the bar savoring spirits
somewhere on the savanna
a leopard reclines in a tree
licking the blood of a fresh kill
terry wonders what it would be like
to be devoured by her

here comes some stray adam
sniffing for fresh pussy
hello beautiful, he says
a silent glare sends him scurrying
tail tucked tight beneath his balls

her gaze sweeps lazily across the room
fixing terry with that big cat stare
peeling away her layers
exposing her naked core
hungry raw grasping

here she comes
slinking through the crowd
sleek and graceful
huntress on the prowl
she stands before terry
a hand extended, inviting
a predator luring her prey
terry takes that hand

they come together on the dance floor
a writhing sweating jungle of bodies
terry lets herself go
losing herself in the music
in this woman
in the heat of her pressing close
soft caress of her breath
depths of dark penetrating eyes

midnight's children

there's something special about nighttime
luminous moon peeking from behind her dark shroud
cool distant light of stars in black satin sky
shadows growing bigger deeper darker
songs of creatures that sleep by day
another world waking up coming alive
wondrous and strange

terry takes a deep breath of crisp night air
beside her this dream of a woman she danced with
walks in flesh and blood striding smoothly
as though night is an old friend

her name means sorrow
this close to her terry can feel
the touch of sadness a hint of melancholy
giving gravity to her graceful steps

i want to show you something, sorrow says
rich throaty voice stroking that tender spot
between terry's ears that makes her shiver
like those stories of tigers bears and wolves
walking upright and talking
sweet tongues hiding sharp teeth

mama's voice warns inside terry's head
be careful terry be careful
there are things that come out at night
things that lurk in the shadows
for tender morsels like you
ghosts demons unclean spirits
wild beasts and humans too

they go the way terry does not know
linking their fingers in the dark
ghost of a grin upon sorrow's lips
devilish twinkle in her eye
together they walk embraced by night

a small token

in the heart of the city
tiny courtyard abandoned by centuries
this secret garden sleeps

in the heart of the garden
winter's breath through lonely tree blows
snow soft as angel down

on the tree in black black thorns
an empty space where a heart would be
grows a red red rose

sorrow brings terry here
plucks the rose tucks it behind her ear
thirsty eyes drinking in
terry's crescent moon smile

kiss

when she first kisses a boy
terry is twelve years old

his name is david cohen
he's nice to her and has pretty eyes
in the parking lot behind the shul
they kiss with their eyes closed
just like in the movies
slobbery and awkward
but kind of nice

there are other boys other kisses

his name is dwayne the freight train
rising star of the football team
he's not jewish but nobody's perfect
his kisses are sweet and tender
the kisses of a fairytale prince
but she can't love him
the way he wants her to

when she first kisses a woman
terry is a sophomore

her name is rachel
a senior with curly red hair
pride flag tattooed on her wrist
on the old couch in the sorority house
she cups terry's face
puts her mouth on top of hers
tongue gently darting
between terry's parting lips
and it feels so right

there are other women other kisses

she who shall not be named
is a wonderful kisser
lips soft supple and oh so sweet
like the flesh of juicy ripe fruit
but sometimes she kisses terry
and it's like she's trying
to steal the breath from her lungs

now there's sorrow
she of the dark x-ray gaze
hungry for terry's nakedness
piercing clothes flesh and other lies
sometimes she kisses
as if her touch will shatter terry
into a million pieces
sometimes she kisses
as if she wants to eat terry alive
sometimes it's both
and terry loves it

the better to know you with

sorrow has eyes like black pearls
on nights like tonight
moon full and stars bright
those pearls seem to gleam
and flicker with eldritch light
all the better to see you with

sorrow has hands like her dad's
wolf's paw hands that can kill
tenderly touch delicate things
rose petals butterfly wings
and terry too
all the better to hold you with

sorrow has lips like heaven
supple flesh melds with terry's perfectly
soft like snowflakes like rose petals
intoxicating
sweeter than wine
all the better to kiss you with

sorrow has a smile like a sphinx
the subtle quirk of her mouth an enigma
luring terry close
to solve the riddle of her
sometimes teeth flash sharp and white
all the better to eat you with

names

sorrow never calls her terry
only tirzah
sultry lips and tongue
savoring each syllable

in sorrow's mouth
her name transforms
terry
plain and simple
tirzah
rare decadent intoxicating
a little bit dangerous
dark chocolate truffle soaked in brandy
with a dash of arsenic

sorrow never calls her terry
only tirzah
smoky hebrew accent
casting a spell on the ear

in sorrow's mouth
her name transforms
terry
nice jewish girl
tirzah
enchanting lovely wild
a little bit dangerous
blood red rose blooming under full moon
hiding sharp thorns

sorrow never calls her terry
only tirzah
rich throaty voice
wrapping her name in a lover's embrace

scar

under a spray of hot water
feather-soft fingers trace
the scar on terry's shoulder
rough ugly mostly numb
what happened?

terry breathes
inhale sorrow one two three
exhale she who shall not be named

odor of burning fabric on a crisp white shirt
iron-shaped scorch the color of a bruise
yelling so much yelling
ruined stupid useless dumb
hiss of hot metal kissing a shoulder blade
white hot pain and curdled screams

terry breathes
inhale sorrow one two three
exhale she who shall not be named

petal-soft kisses press tenderly
upon the ugly old thing
shaped like the tip of an iron
do you want me to kill them for you?

terry does not answer

dreams

night after night terry awakens
from the same dream

enchanting evening by a lake
black velvet sky tinged violet
stars twinkle like sprinkled fairy dust
water's surface mirror smooth
reflects the heavens perfectly

night after night terry awakens
from the same dream

sphere of white light descends
transforms into a humanoid shape
tall and lithe without a face
a ballerina in a tutu of white feathers
holds out a hand inviting

night after night terry awakens
from the same dream

she lays her hand into a soft, warm palm
dances with the woman who has no face
sweeping across the surface of the lake
moving with her in flawless harmony
easier than breathing

night after night terry awakens
from the same dream

sickening crunch of bones snapping
faceless dancer rips in two
hot spray of blood lands in terry's face
from steaming mass of blood and viscera
monster emerges drenched in afterbirth red
eyes glowing like molten gold

night after night terry awakens
from the same dream

grip like iron drags her into a devil dance
spinning spinning spinning
like some infernal cyclone
world a kaleidoscopic blur
barely breathing she hangs on for dear life

night after night terry awakens
from the same dream

gasping for air
wet and throbbing with arousal
she brings herself to climax
conjuring images of eyes like fire
a dance that leaves her breathless
kisses that taste like blood

beware beware

beware terry beware
the monster follows you
in your beloved's shadow

no it's just sorrow
walking beside me
i'm seeing things that's all

beware terry beware
the monster comes for you
wearing your beloved's face

no it's just sorrow
looking at me
a trick of the light that's all

beware terry beware
the monster speaks to you
in your beloved's voice

no it's just sorrow
talking with me
i'm hearing things that's all

beware terry beware
the monster reaches for you
with your beloved's hand

no it's just sorrow
sharing her warmth with me
i'm being silly that's all

Shawn C. Harris

beware terry beware
the monster is kissing you
with your beloved's lips

no it's just sorrow
being tender and sweet
i'm imagining things that's all

beware terry beware
the monster lies in your bed
hidden inside your beloved's skin

no it's just sorrow
keeping me company
a dream mere fantasy that's all

beware terry beware
the monster is carrying you away
in your beloved's arms

no it's just sorrow
taking me to the realm of demons
i'm going home that's all

Book Three:

Sitra Achra

(The Other Side)

the palace

i am a palace of many chambers
majestic and lonely like the ones in fairy tales
i am not some cute saccharine thing
scrubbed clean of blood sex and death
i am old and dark like the original stories
passed grandmother to mother to daughter

the moment tirzah steps into my halls
candles and lanterns ignite (let there be light)
room after room i prepare for her arrival
scents of herbs and spices fill my kitchen
clothes of the perfect size line my wardrobes
she shall be my mistress and i her home

she takes a breath and a lively breeze blows
stirring the drapes banishing stale air
that breath reaches my courtyard
the garden blossoms back to life
trees and flowers shake off the sleep of winter
fountains come alive with the song of water

hidden at the heart of me i have a secret place
behind a red, red door that must never be opened

gifts

sorrow
the monster
sorrow
leaves her gifts

pomegranate of pure silver
shining like a little moon
sits on the dining table
in the place where terry eats
arils of garnet sparkle dark red
like little drops of blood

sorrow
the monster
sorrow
leaves her gifts

cocoon green and smooth
like a tiny coffin made of jade
waits in the garden where terry strolls
night's butterfly emerges
unfurls dark wings spotted with eyes
like the wings of an angel

sorrow
the monster
sorrow
leaves her gifts

red red rose on her pillow
warm and pulsing like a tiny heart
sharp thorn hidden behind the petals
like a stiletto hidden up a sleeve
it lives in the vase on terry's nightstand
where it never wilts

silver candlesticks

baruch atah adonoy
eloheinu melech ha-olam
asher kid'shanu b'mitzvotav v'tzivanu
lehadlik ner shel shabbos

in the dining room of the palace
twin angels clad in white
atop twin towers of gleaming silver
each twin crowned in flame

terry remembers
bubbe's house so full of magic
smelling of challah and old people
silver candlesticks lovingly tarnished

baruch atah adonoy
eloheinu melech ha-olam
borei p'ri hagafen

once upon a time
there were two silver candlesticks
one day these will be yours
bubbe said beaming with pride

once upon a time
terry escaped a dragon's lair
where she abandoned bubbe's
lovely silver candlesticks

baruch atah adonoy
eloheinu melech ha-olam
hamotzi lechem min ha'aretz

her heart cracks open
tears come streaming out
sorrow catches them in her palm
where they turn into diamonds

embraced in holy light
terry says the blessings
for wine and for bread
as bubbe showed her

why why not

why me?
terry asks without asking

why not you?
sorrow says
and silences questions with a kiss

why me?
terry asks without asking

why not you?
sorrow says but she means
must everything be spoken
for it to be real?

why me?
terry asks without asking

why not you?
sorrow says but she means
my heart was barren before
you came and showed me
what wondrous things can grow there

why me?
terry asks without asking

why not you?
sorrow says but she means
because you are you
dayeinu

fragile

brittle snowflakes fall on leaf grass and flower
shatter like glass shards making soft music
that sounds like heartache
in the garden terry listens
thinking of broken things
eggshells toys bones hearts
trust innocence families lives

heady aroma of roses and wild animal
caresses terry's face
sorrow is here

carefully carefully a deadly claw
slices open the back of terry's dress
exposing the scar that lives on her shoulder
terry leans into furnace-hot breath
a lamb bearing its neck to the wolf
terry closes her eyes
safer in the dark of her own making

sorrow whispers, *do not be afraid*
terry melts into the sound of that voice
sweet and smoky like tobacco
like those cigars nana used to smoke

gently gently sorrow touches terry's scar
grazing the edge of discolored patch of skin
lethal talons do not leave a scratch
i will kill the one who did this
if you wish it
do you wish it?
terry does not say

tenderly tenderly sorrow bathes terry's scar
with long lazy laps of her tongue
terry surrenders to primal kisses
with each lick upon that old ugly thing
skin once rough becomes smooth again
and what was numb feels again

hot fat tears leak from terry's eyes
softly softly sorrow licks these too

home

what is home
a number and a street name
some building squatting in the earth
mailbox stuffed with junk mail and bills

this palace of dreams
maze of ever-shifting halls
dancing shadows and eldritch light

what is home
a neighborhood of stone slabs
houses of dust and ashes
tiny, dark rooms cold as corpses

this enchanting garden
roses blooming red as life's blood
trees moving when no one looks

what is home
living dead shambling back and forth
puppets pulled by invisible strings
empty shells walking across a hollow world

this beautiful monster
a prince among she-demons
with the touch of an angel

bloody kisses

in the wilderness beyond
the embrace of the palace
terry hunts for sorrow
seeking signs on paths unknown
demons drool in her wake
but dare not touch

she finds the twitching carcass
of a horned hoofed beast
steam rises from a river of blood
pouring from the severed throat
here sorrow stands naked splashed in red
red on her hands red on her mouth
so horrible so beautiful

sorrow tears out the heart
bites off a piece flashing white canines
brings a morsel to terry's mouth (eat me)
terry tastes the offering
red streak dribbling down her chin (drink me)
they taste each other deeply with lips tongues teeth
dancing on the edge of pleasure and pain

agony and ecstasy

sorrow makes love like an angel

with the caress of her hand
she blesses breast and nipple
with the kisses of her mouth
she worships vulva and clit
delicious agony pierces through her
it burns fills her with heavenly fire
again and again terry cries out
coming apart in sorrow's arms

sorrow fucks like a demon

her kiss searing hellfire
her touch devouring flame
immolating terry from within
relentless fingers lips tongue
tear orgasm after orgasm out of her
as if trying to rip the soul from her body
terry writhing and thrashing
a woman possessed howls in feral ecstasy

warning

sorrow shows her the red red door
(come and see come and see)
and she says unto terry
beyond this door is a secret
you must not look
you must not look lest you die

night after night
blood flows through terry's dreams
a chamber of horrors
filled with cut up corpses
chopped up pieces just like hers
her arms and her legs
her hands and her feet
her head and her torso
her breasts and her cunt
her heart her lungs her womb
and yet
and yet
(come and see come and see)

the red door opens

the red door waits

siren's song in terry's dreams
chanting whispers hissing softly
come and see come and see

the red door waits

terry walks as she sleeps
haunting chthonic halls
come and see come and see

the red door waits

forbidden door stands stop sign red
stop do not enter wrong way
come and see come and see

the red door waits

you must not look, sorrow said
you must not look lest you die
come and see come and see

the red door waits

the red door cracks open
from beyond alien light shines
terry looks and sees and screams

akeidah

the palace has many doors
behind this one lies a hot spring
within its midnight dark walls
diamonds sparkle like stars
sorrow takes terry there

whispering words of blessing
terry immerses herself
warm wet waters embrace her
kissing every part of her
like the waters of the womb

baruch atah adonai eloheinu melech ha-olam
asher kidshanu b'mitzvotav v'tzivanu
al ha-t'vilah

she rises from the water
skin gleaming
anointed in fragrant oils
crown of roses upon her brow
covered in a shroud of white linen

baruch atah adonai eloheinu melech ha-olam
shehecheyanu v'kiyimanu v'higiyanu la-z'man ha-zeh

she's laid on an altar
of moss and leaves and pine needles
inhales the crisp green scent
will it hurt, she asks
yes, says sorrow

long clawed fingers of strange beautiful hands
graze the soft skin of terry's throat
gently wrap around lovely brown neck
and begin to squeeze

shema yisrael adonai eloheinu adonai echad

hineini

i am the one who comes for all
i have come for her
give her the kiss
parting soul from body

hineini, she says
here i am

i call to her
i whisper her name
my voice is dead leaves graveyard dirt
wind scraping against hollow bone

hineini, she says
here i am

i come to her
i spread my wings
wrap her in a cocoon of night
soft and warm as the womb

hineini, she says
here i am

i take her hand
i take the lead
waltz through her every moment
the dance of her life

hineini, she says
here i am

i have always been
close
close as her own shadow
close as her own breath

hineini, she says
here i am

i prepare to deliver unto her my kiss

Book Four:

Galut

(Exile)

awakening

terry wakes up
shrouded in white linen sheets
sterile light shines on sterile surfaces
antiseptic smell not quite masking
the rotten meat stench of sickness and death

mama and dov and izzy
crowd around her bed
gap between mother and brothers
where dad would should be
we are but dust and ashes

outside her window
the angel of death waves at her
then slips into the floor below
a heart monitor flatlines code blue
v'imru amein

changes

terry helps mama chop vegetables
they're making curried goat for shabbos
you've changed, mama says
like a piece of you lives someplace else
i'm still me, terry tells her
but mama just smiles

terry eats dessert at her godmother's house
a slice of chocolate cake dark and moist
something's different about you, sophie says
like something happened to you over there
i'm still me, terry tells her
if you say so, sophie says

terry brings a plate to aunt big helen
fried chicken greens yams cornbread
you ain't the same, big helen says
like you got another face under this one
i'm still me, terry tells her
mmhm, says big helen

red dreams

her dreams flow red

red red rose
soft as velvet fragrant arousing
she reaches for the stem
wicked thorn sinks into her flesh
drawing blood drop drop drop

red red heart
hot and throbbing in her hands
soaking her in life's blood
she sinks her teeth into its flesh
savoring sweet tender meat

red red door
silently opening
(come and see come and see)
a giant red maw
swallowing her in otherworldly light

medusa

tangling coils of nappy hair
writhe atop her head
a nest of snakes

her mouth is filled with poison
her tongue a razor blade
her brother jokes about pms
and milk curdles at her cursing

stretching ear to ear
a smile that chills to the bone
like a tiger bearing its teeth

her gaze is winter sharp and cold
some douchebag tells her, *smile!*
her glare freezes his face in mute horror
as though he were turned to stone

lurking behind dark doe eyes
a wild and dangerous thing
not of this world

breathe

on the other side
of a winding midnight road
a truck lumbering closer closer
halogen eyes flood her car with light
bright and terrible just like

just like

the red red door
like a headstone drenched in blood
opening slowly
(come and see come and see)
drenching her in that awful light

will it hurt
yes

in the midnight darkness
of terry's bedroom
a black and white movie playing
smooth flat face of the tv screen
shining with unnatural light just like

just like

the red red door
like a face blood-soaked and serene
cracking open
(come and see come and see)
spilling forbidden light

and she can't breathe
she can't breathe
she can't
breathe

the visit

she saw dad the other day

it was the middle of the afternoon
soul music playing in the basement
his favorite motown hits
down down down terry went

and there he was

hunched over his workbench
gazing at all his unfinished projects
as though he never left

then she remembered

dad still and cold in a hospital bed
wrapped up in white linen like a mummy
mama's sobs as she clung to his corpse
pine box swallowed up by cool dark earth

but there he was

turning around and giving her this look
that seemed to ask, *what are you doing here*
as though she were the ghost

and then he was gone

chrysalis

a princess asleep
inside a crystal coffin
shining with its own gentle light
iridescent as a cicada's wing
slumbering for one night or a hundred years
weaving whole lives from the stuff of dreams

in this dream her name is terry
descending into the bowels of the world
into this cave where the coffin lies
heaves the lid open and finds herself
lying on a bed of satin
she touches this other terry and feels
not wood or plastic but living flesh

closed eyes fly open
hands inhumanly strong grab terry
there is a kiss tart and heady like wine
flare of pain as teeth sink into her lip
blood trickles into terry's mouth
and she likes it

terry awakens
sting of pain clinging to her lip
taste of salt and iron faint in her mouth
slightly swollen as if something bit her there

déjà vu

there are moments
when she feels the kiss
of wind on her cheek
soft and swift
comes the fragrance of roses
the core of her clenches
yearning
for a time
for a place
(for someone)
she knows only in dreams

monster's lullaby

there's a monster at your window
whispering your name
voice thick and smoky as autumn fog
calling you

come away come away
to the other side of the red red door
come away come away
to the other side where the monsters dwell

there's a monster in your room
whispering your name
a taloned hand extends silently
inviting you

come away come away
to the other side of the red red door
come away come away
to the other side where the monsters dwell

there's a monster in your bed
whispering your name
smelling of wild animal and roses
begging you

come away come away
to the other side of the red red door
come away come away
to the other side where the monsters dwell

Shawn C. Harris

four answers

why is this night not like all other nights?

on all other nights
i wait for her to come
patient as the angel of death
whispering to her in her dreams
come and see come and see

on this night
there is a change in the air
mighty queer wind sweeps through
bending branches rustling leaves
on pins and needles i wait

why is this night not like all other nights?

on all other nights
she comes to these woods dark and deep
walking in her sleep as if possessed
puppet of skin and bone
dancing on ghostly strings

on this night
she comes awake eyes wide open
threading through shadows of ancient trees
night breeze like breath of demons blows
terry shudders suddenly cold

why is this night not like all other nights?

on all other nights
i am crawling with vines
winding serpentine across my face
like varicose veins in ruddy skin
deep crimson peeking through the green

on this night
carved deep into my wood she finds her name
letters curved like a woman's nakedness
sharp edges worn smooth by time
as though her name was always there

why is this night not like all other nights?

on all other nights
she comes before me speaking nonsense
dreaming gibberish falling from her tongue
dad empty shells ok
roses monster sorrow yes

on this night
she says, *hineini here i am*
slowly slowly i open wide
(you must not look lest you die)
swallowing her in unearthly light

reawakening

on the other side of the red door
a heart beats once twice thrice
breathing starts with a gasp
dark brown eyes fly open

terry awakens
wearing a white linen sheet
lying on a cold stone slab
red red rose clutched to her breast

palace falling apart piece by piece
the carcass of some gargantuan beast
stale air stinks faintly of decay
(we are but dust and ashes v'imru amein)

the garden has gone barren
wasteland of weeds and dust
littered with tiny animal skulls
a womb bearing death instead of life

a marble statue in sorrow's likeness
wrapped in brittle brown vines
every detail perfectly chiseled
but breath and heartbeat

terry caresses a cold hard cheek
lips of flesh meet lips of stone
sweet kiss mingling with bitter tears
warm soft mouth kisses back

clawed fingers gingerly stroke terry's face
as though a touch would turn her to ash
tirzah, sorrow asks voice quivering
terry answers, *here i am*

The Red Door

Book Five:

Teshuvah

(Return)

a wedding

today there is a wedding
people stream toward the chuppah on the hill
small white candles clasped in their hands
flames flickering fragile as life

today the bride is chava
she is sarah and she is rivkah
she is leah and she is rachel
shining in her gown like a white star

today the spirits of ancestors
gather and follow the procession
wrapped in their burial shrouds
sending sudden chills into those they walk through

unanswered

hey this is terry
you know what to do

hey baby it's mama
i don't want nothing
just calling to see
how you doing

beeeep!

hey this is terry
you know what to do

hey terry it's izzy
just got a new phone
did you hear
about this new anime
it's about this girl
who goes to another world
to live with this demon
seems like your kinda thing
anyway call me back

beeeep!

hey this is terry
you know what to do

hey sis it's dov
did you ever get that necklace
dad bought you
he was gonna give it to you
for your birthday this year
but then he
you know
let me know either way
ok bye

beeeep!

hey this is terry
you know what to do

hey terry it's me again
you talk to ma yet
she been trying to call you
can you call her back
or send her a text
or something
bye

beeeep!

hey this is terry
you know what to do

terry it's mama
i been trying to call you
where are you
is everything ok
call me soon as you get this

beeeep!

hey this is terry
you know what to do

beeeep!

the voice mailbox of the person
you're trying to reach
is full please try again later

kiddushin

a courtyard vast and verdant
its heart a cluster of four trees
branches entwined like lovers' arms
wrapped in roses red as ram's blood
a chuppah of flowers and thorns

under the chuppah of flowers and thorns
princely she-demon and her human bride
exchange matching gold rings
matching glances ravenous
promising bestial delights

under the chuppah of flowers and thorns
quaking rabbi recites the seven blessings
wine shared from a silver cup
sweeter than true love's kiss
glass wrapped in cloth stomped to pieces
chorus of unearthly voices cry, *mazel tov!*

nightmare

on this side of the red door
a wedding feast of otherworldly splendor
lavish beyond dreams of greed
guests parading aristocratic finery
wine flowing like water, decadent red
in the place for newlyweds terry sits
dark and lovely as the queen of sheba
sneaking heated glances to her wife

on this side of the red door
the air goes chill and sharp
shadows shift in the moonlight
monsters come out of hiding
from the guests' human guises
horns and cloven hooves
wings and taloned feet
eyes glow feral yellow and infernal red
grinning mouths full of sharp teeth

on this side of the red door
she who shall not be named is brought forth
her feet forced into iron shoes
red hot like simmering rage
hiss of hot metal biting into skin
smoke rises from blistering feet
smell of seared flesh and melting fat
floating up to heaven
a burnt offering

on this side of the red door
the monsters chant, *dance! dance! dance!*
clapping stomping laughing
she who shall not be named
kicks up her burning heels
spinning and spinning
wickedly bewitching
like a dreidel on fire careening wildly
to a devil's frenzied fiddling
as terry watches clapping and smiling

song of tirzah

i am my beloved's
and my beloved is mine

give me the kisses of her mouth
how delightful her taste
her lips are milk and honey
her kiss is like wine

i am my beloved's
and my beloved is mine

her desire is for me
for i am dark and comely
a rose and its thorn
nesting between her breasts

i am my beloved's
and my beloved is mine

strong and supple is her embrace
a tree bearing ripe fruit
i delight to lie in her shade
her fruit is sweet to my mouth

i am my beloved's
and my beloved is mine

give me the kisses of her mouth
her lips are pure sweetness
her love is stronger than wine
i am drunk on the taste of her

i am my beloved's
and my beloved is mine

metamorphosis

a change is coming
terry can feel it
in the embrace of her beloved sorrow
riding wave after wave of bliss
nails sink into sorrow's flesh drawing blood
avian cries of ecstasy pierce the night

a change is coming
clawing out of her from the inside
splitting her apart from within
there is pain and screaming and so much blood
piece by piece she sheds her human skin
husk of her old self a heap of bloody shreds

a new terry emerges
glistening red from the afterbirth
beautiful horrible magnificent
sorrow worships her with her eyes
and with her mouth suckles a bloody nipple
as though tasting divine nectar

forgetting

the mortal world is starting to forget her

friends acquaintances extended family
draw a blank where a face should be
no longer remember the sound of her voice
did she like to sing
did she talk a lot or hardly at all
and what was her name again
tina toni terry tammy
something starting with t

the world is starting to forget

there are still signs of her
scraps of a life left behind
dried petals of a red red rose
pressed between pages of a novel
margins of an old notebook
filled with sketches of red red doors

world starting to forget

everyone except her mother
who will remember her always
and never forget
is this a blessing
or a curse

bittersweet

perhaps she has wistful moments
moments as gentle as mist
when she misses
her brother's laugh
her mother's hugs
little things from the mortal world
for there is always bitter with sweet

perhaps in such moments
these moments fleeting as wind
when she misses her old world
her old life
her old self
she holds sorrow closer
drawing her warmth inside
to fill the tiny cracks in her heart

a mother's lament

she's gone
far far away
beyond this world
of dust and ashes

they think she's dead
but that is not so
my little girl lives
this i know

she's blissfully happy
in my dreams
living like a princess
and married i think

how will i live
with no one
to live for
but myself

perhaps
i shall garden again
roses i think
red as red can be

come and see

there is inside
each of us
a red door
waiting
come and see come and see
do you
see it

there is inside
each of us
a red door
calling
come and see come and see
do you
hear it

there is inside
each of us
a red door
opening
to the other side
come and see come and see
do you
feel it

there is inside
each of us
a red door
leading to secret places
within
beyond
come and see come and see
do you

About the Author

Shawn C. Harris (she/they) is an author, playwright, educator, and gigantic nerd who appreciates art and media that revel in the chthonic side of imagination. THE RED DOOR is her debut poetry collection and was a semi-finalist for the Cave Canem Poetry Prize. Her nonfiction has been featured in *Tablet* and *TribeHerald*. She currently lives among her extended family in Virginia, where she was born and raised.

CPSIA information can be obtained
at www.ICGtesting.com
Printed in the USA
BVHW042120030922
646136BV00007BA/433